THE POETRY OF PLUTONIUM

The Poetry of Plutonium

Walter the Educator

Silent King Books

SILENT KING BOOKS

SKB

Copyright © 2024 by Walter the Educator

All rights reserved. No part of this book may be reproduced in any manner whatsoever without written permission except in the case of brief quotations embodied in critical articles and reviews.

First Printing, 2024

Disclaimer
This book is a literary work; poems are not about specific persons, locations, situations, and/or circumstances unless mentioned in a historical context. This book is for entertainment and informational purposes only. The author and publisher offer this information without warranties expressed or implied. No matter the grounds, neither the author nor the publisher will be accountable for any losses, injuries, or other damages caused by the reader's use of this book. The use of this book acknowledges an understanding and acceptance of this disclaimer.

"Earning a degree in chemistry changed my life!"
— Walter the Educator

dedicated to all the chemistry lovers, like myself, across the world

PLUTONIUM

Rare and profound,

PLUTONIUM

Lies plutonium, mysterious, yet renowned.

PLUTONIUM

Born in the fires of cosmic creation,

PLUTONIUM

Its allure and dangers stir fascination.

PLUTONIUM

With atomic number ninety-four it claims,

PLUTONIUM

A legacy shrouded in enigmatic flames.

PLUTONIUM

Man-made, yet possessing atomic might,

PLUTONIUM

Plutonium dances in nuclear light.

PLUTONIUM

Within its core, a symphony of decay,

PLUTONIUM

Radiant particles in disarray.

PLUTONIUM

Its isotopes, a spectral array,

PLUTONIUM

Unveil secrets in a radioactive ballet.

PLUTONIUM

From the labs of science to the halls of war,

PLUTONIUM

Plutonium's story, we cannot ignore.

PLUTONIUM

A catalyst for change, for good or ill,

PLUTONIUM

Its destiny intertwined with human will.

PLUTONIUM

In reactors, it fuels the modern age,

PLUTONIUM

Powering cities on history's stage.

PLUTONIUM

Yet its shadow looms, a specter of dread,

PLUTONIUM

In the aftermath of conflicts, lives led.

PLUTONIUM

Beneath the earth, in chambers deep,

PLUTONIUM

Plutonium slumbers, a guarded keep.

PLUTONIUM

For its potency wields a double-edged sword,

PLUTONIUM

A cautionary tale of science explored.

PLUTONIUM

But beyond its role in human affairs,

PLUTONIUM

Plutonium whispers of cosmic affairs.

PLUTONIUM

Forged in the crucible of exploding stars,

PLUTONIUM

It traversed space, crossing cosmic bars.

PLUTONIUM

From supernovae's fiery embrace,

PLUTONIUM

Plutonium journeyed through time and space.

PLUTONIUM

Carrying the essence of distant suns,

PLUTONIUM

To Earth's embrace, its journey done.

PLUTONIUM

In the hands of poets, it finds new voice,

PLUTONIUM

A muse for musings, a chance to rejoice.

PLUTONIUM

For in its essence, there lies a tale,

PLUTONIUM

Of boundless wonder and cosmic trail.

PLUTONIUM

So let us ponder, with reverence and awe,

PLUTONIUM

Plutonium's story, both beauty and flaw.

PLUTONIUM

A testament to human curiosity,

PLUTONIUM

And the mysteries of the cosmic sea.

PLUTONIUM

As we navigate this world of science and lore,

PLUTONIUM

Let us tread lightly, and explore.

PLUTONIUM

For in the depths of plutonium's glow,

PLUTONIUM

Lies the promise of knowledge, both high and low.

PLUTONIUM

ABOUT THE CREATOR

Walter the Educator is one of the pseudonyms for Walter Anderson. Formally educated in Chemistry, Business, and Education, he is an educator, an author, a diverse entrepreneur, and he is the son of a disabled war veteran. "Walter the Educator" shares his time between educating and creating. He holds interests and owns several creative projects that entertain, enlighten, enhance, and educate, hoping to inspire and motivate you.

> Follow, find new works, and stay up to date
> with Walter the Educator™
> at WaltertheEducator.com

www.ingramcontent.com/pod-product-compliance
Lightning Source LLC
LaVergne TN
LVHW012049070526
838201LV00082B/3868